ENERGY TRANSFERS

From
Crashing Waves
to
Music Download

An Energy Journey Through the World of Sound

Andrew Solway

heinemann
raintree

Edited by Linda Staniford and Anthony Wacholtz
Designed by Steve Mead
Original illustrations © Capstone Global Library 2015
Illustrated by HL Studios
Picture research by Eric Gohl
Production by Helen McCreath
Originated by Capstone Global Library Ltd
Printed and bound in China by CTPS

18 17 16 15 14
10 9 8 7 6 5 4 3 2 1

Library of Congress Cataloging-in-Publication Data

Solway, Andrew, author.
  From windy day to music download : an energy journey through the world of sound / Andrew Solway.
    pages cm.—(Energy journeys)
  Summary: "Each book in this series follows a packet of energy along a journey. Each stage of the journey is described in a short chapter, and we learn what alternative paths the energy might have taken along the way. This book shows how the energy in wind is turned into a music download. It explains the science behind sound, how it can be measured, recorded and stored, what happens in a recording studio, and how our ears hear sound. The topics covered are illustrated with experiments, amazing facts and scientific discoveries."—Provided by publisher.
  Includes bibliographical references and index.
  ISBN 978-1-4846-0883-8 (hb)—ISBN 978-1-4846-0888-3 (pb) —ISBN 978-1-4846-0898-2 (ebook) 1. Sound—Juvenile literature. 2. Power resources—Juvenile literature. I. Title.

QC225.5.S647 2015
534—dc23   2014015712

This book has been officially leveled by using the F&P Text Level Gradient™ Leveling System.

Acknowledgments

We would like to thank the following for permission to reproduce photographs: Corbis: Imaginechina, 32; Courtesy of Lisa Park: 43; ESA: Guus Schoonewille, 37; Getty Images: Moment Open/Fotografía de juandevillalba, 21; Glow Images: Michael Peuckert, 20; iStockphotos: Doctor_bass, 10–11, jophil, 24, PlushStudios, 34; Library of Congress: 31 (bottom); Newscom: Getty Images/AFP/Radek Mica, 22, Minden Pictures/Michael Durham, 13, picture-alliance/dpa/Nicolas Armer, 41, Westend61 GmbH/Martin Rietze, 5; Science Source: Andrew Lambert Photography, 35, David McCarthy, 25, Pascal Goetgheluck, 42, Paul Wootton, 31 (top), Ted Kinsman, 7, 33; Shutterstock: Anna Omelchenko, 16, Anton Gvozdikov, 36, Bastian Kienitz, 6, bikeriderlondon, cover (bottom), 4, BlueRingMedia, 38, Carlos Wunderlin, 18, Darrin Henry, 28, discpicture, 17, Doug James, 30, Éthan Daniels, 19, nattanan726, 39, Wade Vaillancourt, 40, Zacarias Pereira da Mata, cover (top), 8–9; SuperStock: Cultura Limited, 23.

We would like to thank Patrick O'Mahony for his help in the preparation of this book.

Every effort has been made to contact copyright holders of material reproduced in this book. Any omissions will be rectified in subsequent printings if notice is given to the publisher.

All the Internet addresses (URLs) given in this book were valid at the time of going to press. However, due to the dynamic nature of the Internet, some addresses may have changed, or sites may have changed or ceased to exist since publication. While the author and publisher regret any inconvenience this may cause readers, no responsibility for any such changes can be accepted by either the author or the publisher.

Contents

Discover amazing facts about sound.

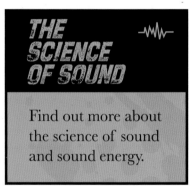

THE SCIENCE OF SOUND

Find out more about the science of sound and sound energy.

SOUND FIRSTS

Learn more about sound inventions and discoveries.

1ST

Some words are shown in bold, **like this**. You can find out what they mean by looking in the glossary.

What Is Energy?

We use the word "energy" in all kinds of ways. If you are always doing things, people say you have lots of energy. You can eat energy bars to provide the fuel to keep you active. Energy companies supply **electricity** *and fuel for heating homes, offices, schools, and factories.*

These examples involve different types of energy. Movement is a type of energy called **kinetic energy**. Energy bars and other fuels are stores of chemical energy. Electricity is a type of energy that can flow through cables and wires. We can use it to power lights, heaters, radios, televisions, computers, drills, lawnmowers, and many other devices.

THE SCIENCE OF SOUND

Fuels, energy bars, springs, rubber bands, a book on a shelf—these are all types of stored, or **potential energy**. Fuels and foods have **chemical potential energy**. Springs and rubber bands have **elastic potential energy**. A book on a shelf, or a skateboard at the top of a slope, has **gravitational potential energy**.

➤ Sprinters convert the chemical potential energy from their food into kinetic energy.

In August 1883, the volcano on the island of Krakatoa, Indonesia, erupted in a series of huge explosions. The explosions were heard 2,200 miles (3,500 kilometers) away, in Australia. The sound took nearly three hours to travel this distance.

Making things happen

Energy is about making things happen. If there were no energy, the world would be cold, dark, still—and lifeless. There would be no life here at all. Some types of energy travel from place to place. Light can travel billions of miles across space. Electricity travels through cables. Sound is another kind of energy that travels. If someone shouts, you can hear it across the street. Some sounds travel hundreds or even thousands of miles.

▲ Krakatoa is still an active volcano. However, recent eruptions have been much smaller than the massive eruption in 1883.

Indestructible energy

Energy doesn't last forever, does it? Batteries don't last forever, and cars run out of fuel. But, in fact, energy really *does* last forever. Scientists have found that, if you look carefully enough, energy does not disappear altogether. It may **transform** into other kinds of energy. Energy is never created or destroyed. This is the law of the **conservation of energy**.

▲ The candle wax is the fuel that keeps the flame going.

How is energy conserved?

Two examples will help to explain this. You make a cup of hot chocolate, but then a friend drops by and you forget about it. By the time you remember, you have a cup of cold chocolate. In this case, the heat energy from the chocolate hasn't disappeared. It has gradually spread out into the surroundings, making the air in the room a tiny bit warmer.

Here is another example. You take a mug off the shelf, but it slips and drops. Luckily, it doesn't break. The mug on the shelf had gravitational potential energy. When you dropped it, this turned to kinetic energy. When the mug hit the floor, some of the kinetic energy became sound: CRASH! Most of the rest became heat energy. The mug and the floor are now slightly warmer than before.

▲ The tightly stretched skin of the balloon has elastic potential energy. When the balloon bursts, it makes a loud "'POP!" Most of the potential energy has been transformed into sound.

Although energy is never lost completely, it can stop being useful. Once the energy from your hot chocolate has spread through the air, it is hard to even measure. You can't really do anything with this energy.

What Is Sound?

Our energy journey starts on a stormy night in a harbor. It is too dark to see, but there is lots of noise. A wooden shutter bangs against a window frame, and a metal garbage can clatters down the street. The harbor is full of tapping and clanking noises made by cables and pulleys hitting masts. The wind wails and whistles through the rigging of the boats. And all the time there is the hiss of rain and the crash of waves on the harbor wall.

Sound basics

So, what is sound, and how is it produced? Sound is a type of **wave** energy. Sound waves are **vibrations**. Usually we hear sounds in the air, but sound can also travel through liquids and solids.

Waves in water can range in height from tiny ripples to huge breakers. Sound waves can also vary in size, or **amplitude**. A large-amplitude sound wave is loud. Small-amplitude waves are quiet.

The **wavelength** of a wave is the distance from the top of one wave to the top of the next. In sound, wavelength is related to the **pitch** of the sound. High-pitched sounds have a short wavelength. Lower-pitched sounds have a longer wavelength.

▼ One of the main sounds of a storm in a harbor is the waves crashing against the harbor walls.

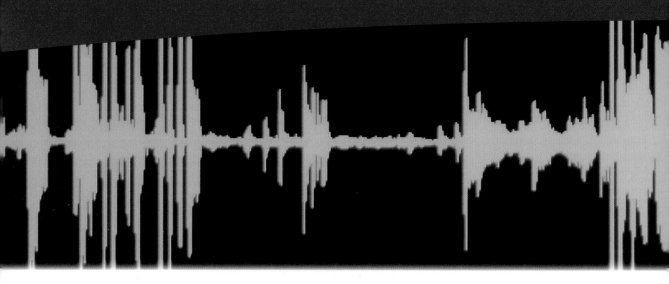

Looking at sounds

What do sound waves look like? To find out, we can use an instrument called an **oscilloscope**. This shows sound waves on a screen. If you look at a very pure musical note on an oscilloscope, it shows as a regular up and down trace. If you change the note to a higher pitch, the waves get closer together. This makes sense, because we have already seen that a high-pitched sound has a shorter wavelength than a low-pitched sound.

If you make the pure note louder, the waves on the screen get taller. With a quiet note, the waves are shorter. Again, this ties in with what we know. The loudness of a sound is connected to the amplitude of the wave.

Real sounds

If we look at the sound waves produced by real musical instruments, they do not look like the simple waves on the oscilloscope. This is because a real musical instrument does not produce a single, pure note. In addition to the main note, the sound includes higher and lower notes called **harmonics**. These are not as loud as the main note, but they change the character of the sound. This helps to explain why a note played on a piano has a different quality than the same note played on a violin. The instruments have different harmonics.

When several instruments are playing together, and the notes are changing in pitch and loudness, it becomes impossible to see the individual sound waves that make up the music.

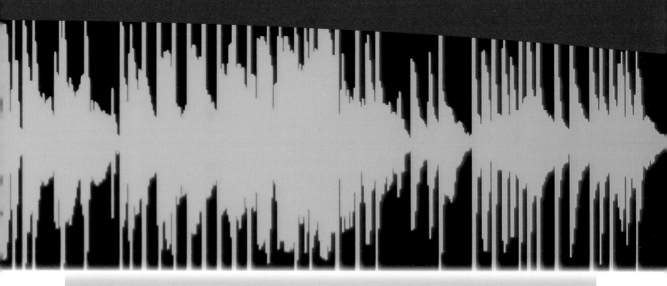

▲ This sound trace shows a real piece of music. The sound does not have a smooth wave shape, but it is possible to see where the sounds are louder and where they are quieter.

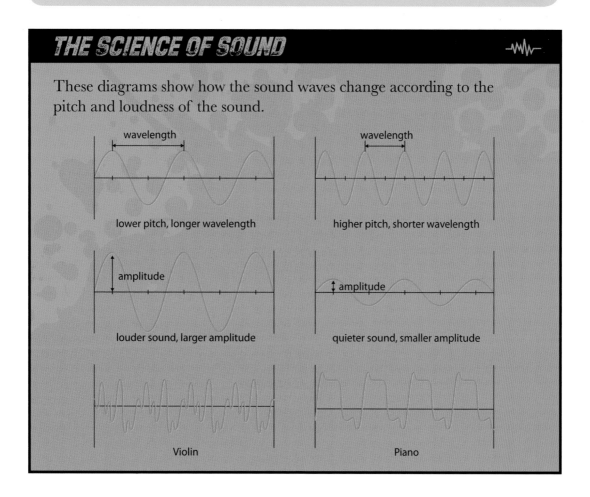

THE SCIENCE OF SOUND

These diagrams show how the sound waves change according to the pitch and loudness of the sound.

wavelength

lower pitch, longer wavelength

wavelength

higher pitch, shorter wavelength

amplitude

louder sound, larger amplitude

amplitude

quieter sound, smaller amplitude

Violin

Piano

The causes of noises

Now that we understand more about sound, let's look again at the storm on page 8. How were the different sounds in the storm made?

Winds are air movements. In a strong wind, the air pushes other objects and makes them move, too. The bangs and clatters are caused by the wind making one object hit another, such as a shutter hitting a window frame or a cable hitting a mast. As the objects hit, they produce sound vibrations. The noises in the rigging are caused by the wind making the tight cables and ropes vibrate.

THE SCIENCE OF SOUND

This table shows the decibel levels of some sounds.

Decibels	Type of sound
0	quietest sounds—threshold (point) of human hearing
10	rustling leaves
20	whisper
40	quiet room in a house
60	normal conversation
70	average street noise; loud telephone
80	busy street traffic
90	vacuum cleaner
100	electric saw
110	large orchestra: front-row seats
120	loud rock music; jet airliner
130	military jet—threshold (point) of pain

The wind also causes the large waves in the sea. As the waves hit the shore, some of their energy is transformed into loud, crashing sounds.

Measuring sound

Loud sounds can damage our ears, so it is important to measure how loud sounds are. The volume of a sound is measured in **decibels** (dB). The quietest sound our ears can hear is measured as 0 dB. The level at which sounds start to hurt our ears (the threshold of pain) is 130 dB.

The pitch of a sound is usually measured as its **frequency**. This is a measure of how many sound vibrations happen per second. The unit of frequency is **hertz** (Hz). The lowest-pitched sounds that humans can hear are around 20 Hz. The highest-pitched are about 20,000 Hz. Sounds that are higher pitched than this are called **ultrasound**.

Animals such as dogs, cats, mice, whales, and bats can hear sounds that are higher pitched than the ones we can hear. Bats can hear sounds as high as 200,000 Hz.

▲ Bats use a kind of sonar for hunting at night. They make high-pitched sounds and use the echoes to help them detect flying insects in the dark.

MAKING SOUNDS WITH RUBBER BANDS

To make a sound, all you need to do is to make something vibrate. In this experiment, you will use rubber bands to make vibrations.

You will need:
- **a cardboard box**
- **scissors**
- **packing tape or other strong tape**
- **four rubber bands**
- **a pencil or pen.**

Making it work

1 If you have a cardboard box with flaps, cut about 1 inch (3 centimeters) of cardboard from two of the flaps, so that when you shut it, you have a rectangular hole in the middle.

2 Tape the flaps shut, leaving the hole uncovered.

3 Put the rubber bands around the box so that they run along the length of the hole.

4 Insert a pencil or pen under the rubber bands at one end, about 1 inch (3 centimeters) from the edge of the box. Your guitar is now ready to play!

Try some experiments

By experimenting with your guitar, you should be able to answer these questions.

- Does a tight rubber band make a higher note or a lower note than a loose one?
- If you shorten a "string" by putting your finger on it, does this make a higher or a lower note?

Try pressing your fingers on the "strings" at different places. With a little trial and error, you can mark places on the box where you can get particular notes. Then you can play tunes on your guitar!

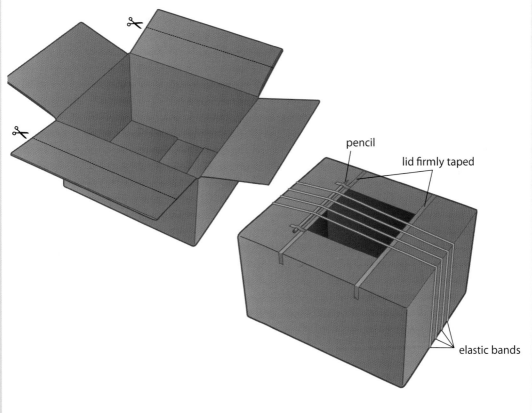

pencil

lid firmly taped

elastic bands

▲ This diagram shows you how to make a box guitar.

What Does Lightning Sound Like?

We started our journey with a storm in a harbor. Now the storm is getting worse. There are even darker clouds approaching, lit up by lightning flashes. As the clouds get closer, the lighting makes bright, forked trails. Each lightning flash is accompanied by a big crash of thunder.

What is lightning?

Lightning bolts are basically huge electrical sparks. We normally think of lightning as flashing down from the clouds to Earth, but lightning flashes can also leap from Earth to the clouds, and between different clouds. The sparks are caused by differences in electrical **charge** between Earth and the clouds.

➤ Lightning bolts are giant electrical sparks ripping through the air.

Air is not a good **conductor** of electricity. In fact, it is a good **insulator**. For this reason, it takes a massive amount of electrical energy to make a spark rip through the air. A lightning bolt can contain up to a billion **volts** of electricity.

The sound of lightning

If you put a lot of electric current though a wire, it heats up. A lightning bolt is a massive amount of electricity, so where it passes, some of the energy is transformed into heat. The air gets incredibly hot. The super-hot air expands extremely quickly, pushing out in a high-speed pressure wave. Some of the energy of the expanding air is transformed into sound. We hear this as the crash of thunder.

▲ The filament in an old-fashioned lightbulb resists the flow of electricity. When the electricity is turned on, the filament gets extremely hot. In a similar way, the air gets hot when lightning flashes pass through it.

The speed of sound

When a thunderstorm is directly overhead, you hear the sound of the thunder at the same time you see the lightning flash. But as the storm moves away, the sound of the thunder begins to come after the lightning flash. Why is this?

SOUND FIRSTS

1ST

The first aircraft to go faster than the speed of sound was *Bell XS-1*, flown by U.S. Air Force pilot Chuck Yeager on October 14, 1947. On October 15, 1997, the car Thrust SSC reached a speed of 763 miles per hour (1,228 kilometers per hour). It was the first land vehicle to go faster than the speed of sound.

▲ When an aircraft or other vehicle goes faster than the speed of sound, there is a very loud noise called a **sonic boom**. This is caused by a **shock wave** in front of the vehicle. The white cloud around this aircraft shows that it is about to go **supersonic**.

▲ Because the speed of sound is faster in water, sounds can travel farther. The calls of humpbacked whales can travel hundreds of miles.

The explanation is connected with the different speeds of light and sound. Light travels very, very quickly. In one second, light can travel seven times around the world! So, when a storm is a few miles away, the lightning flashes reach your eyes in a fraction of a second.

Sound travels much more slowly than light. The speed of sound in air at 59 degrees Fahrenheit (15 degrees Celsius) is 761 miles per hour (1,225 kilometers per hour), or about around half a mile (1 kilometer) every three seconds. So, if a storm is a few miles away, the sound of thunder takes several seconds to reach your ears.

Different materials

When we talk about the speed of sound, we usually mean how quickly sound travels through air. In other materials, sound travels at different speeds. In water, for instance, sound travels over four times quicker than in air.

Even in air, the speed of sound varies. Sound travels quicker on a hot day than on a cold day, because the speed of sound increases with temperature.

Alternative journeys

We have already seen that lightning creates heat as it travels through the air. When lightning hits the ground, most of the remaining energy also becomes heat. In sandy soil, a lightning strike can melt the sand and turn it into a glass-like material. This creates root-like glass structures known as **fulgurites**.

DID YOU KNOW?

Many fulgurites have been found in the Sahara Desert in Africa. This is strong evidence that, in the past, there were many thunderstorms in the Sahara region.

▲ These are fulgurites on sandy cliffs in the Cape Verde Islands, off the coast of Africa. When lightning strikes the sandy soil, the sand becomes so hot that it melts and forms glass.

SOUND FIRSTS

The American inventor Benjamin Franklin invented the first lightning rod, in 1749. He attached a pointed brass rod to the top of a building. Later, a wire was added to conduct the lightning safely into the ground.

Lightning strikes

Lightning usually strikes the highest structure in an area, and often this is a tree. Sometimes the lightning runs down the outside of the tree and causes little damage. But sometimes a lightning strike heats up the sap that runs through the heart of the tree. The sap expands and blows the tree apart.

Lightning strikes can also cause damage to tall buildings. However, most large buildings are protected by lightning conductors. These provide a route for the lightning to travel down into the ground without damaging the building.

Occasionally, people are hit directly by lightning. However, death from a lightning strike is very rare. A study in the United States showed that the chances of dying this way are about one in four million.

▲ Tall structures like these skyscrapers attract lightning strikes. It is important for tall buildings to have lightning conductors to safely carry away the electrical charge.

CAN YOU BREAK THE SOUND BARRIER?

You may not get the chance to fly in a supersonic jet or drive a record-breaking car. But it is possible that you could break the sound barrier in your own home—with a towel!

> **You will need:**
> - a small bath towel or dish towel
> - patience!

In the past, and today, many cowboys and ranchers have used bullwhips and stockwhips when herding cattle. When a whip is flicked, it makes a loud cracking noise. This helps to keep the cattle moving during a cattle drive.

Experiments in the 1950s showed that when a bullwhip cracks, the tip of the whip is moving faster than sound. The cracking noise is the sonic boom made as the tip breaks the sound barrier.

In the 1990s, a group of students at the North Carolina School of Science and Mathematics, in Durham, North Carolina, carried out experiments in "snapping" towels. They took high-speed videos to see if, when you "snap" a towel, the tip of the towel moves faster than the speed of sound. The results suggested that this might happen in some cases.

▲ There are whip-cracking competitions in some countries. This girl is competing in a competition in the Czech Republic.

Making it work

Hold one corner of the towel in one hand, and the opposite corner in the other hand. Twirl the towel around itself to make a loose "rope." Pull it taut, then let go with one hand and flick the towel forward with the other. With practice, you can make the towel "snap" as you flick it. Wetting the snapping corner of your towel helps to make a better snapping noise. If you get a really good snap from your towel, the tip could be going supersonic!

▲ Practicing towel-snapping can be fun, but be careful not to hit other people. A snapping towel can be very painful.

How Do We Capture Sounds?

As the storm begins to drop, a group of musicians arrives to make a recording. They want to record the wind and thunder as part of a new song they have written. The musicians set up microphones to record the noise of the storm.

➤ This ball of fur is actually an outside broadcast microphone. The furry cover cuts down the noise of the wind and allows other sounds to be heard.

Capturing sound

Microphones are devices designed to capture sounds. At the heart of all microphones is a sheet of thin material called a **diaphragm**. When sound waves hit the diaphragm, they cause it to vibrate. The microphone then turns the vibrations of the diaphragm into "vibrations," or oscillations, in an electric current. This is called an **electrical signal**.

One type of microphone is called a dynamic microphone. This relies on the fact that if you move a magnet inside a coil of wire, the movement causes an electric current to flow. In a dynamic microphone, a coil of wire is attached to the diaphragm. As the diaphragm vibrates, the coil vibrates, too. In the middle of the coil, there is a magnet. This is not attached to the diaphragm, so it doesn't vibrate. As the coil vibrates, it moves past the magnet, producing a changing current in the wire. This is the electric signal.

DID YOU KNOW?

Researchers at Ludwig Maximilian University, in Munich, Germany, may have created the world's smallest microphone. They found that they could make a gold particle, just 60 billionths of a meter long (1 meter equals 3.3 feet), vibrate in response to sound waves. Researchers think that these "nano-ears" could be used to listen to the sounds made by bacteria and other microbes.

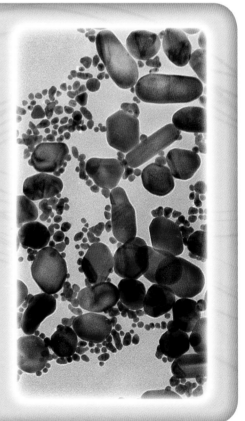

➤ The "nano-ear" is made from a single tiny gold particle like those shown here. The particles are magnified 215,000 times.

How does digital recording work?

Once a microphone has captured a sound, it has to be stored somehow. Today, it is most likely to be stored as **digital information** on an audio recorder or a computer.

The sound signal from a microphone is **analog**. This means that it changes continuously. The electrical signal will be a type of wave, like the original sound.

Let's say we draw the sound signal from the microphone as a wave, like this:

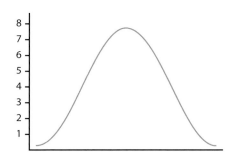

Now let's say we measure the height of the wave at 11 different places, like this:

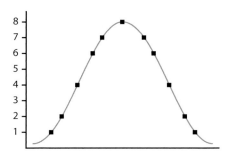

We would get a string of numbers like this: 1, 2, 4, 6, 7, 8, 7, 6, 4, 2, 1. This is a very simple **digital signal**. If you drew the numbers as a bar graph, it would look like this:

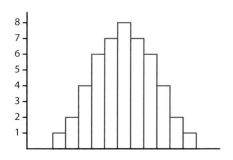

This is a rough copy of the original analog signal, as you can see when you match up the two graphs, like this:

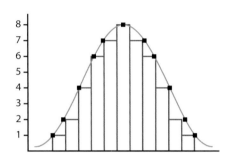

In a real digital signal, the analog signal is **sampled** (measured) thousands of times per second. The result is that the digital signal is almost exactly the same as the analog signal:

Binary numbers

Did you know that a computer can't count to 10? It can't even count to 2! A computer can only recognize two numbers, 0 and 1. This is because a computer stores information as a series of "ons" (1) or "offs" (0). It uses a special counting system, known as **binary**, to store all numbers.

So, in a computer or a digital audio recorder, digital signals are not stored as numbers, but as a long string of "0s" and "1s."

The first eight binary numbers are shown in the table below.

So, on the computer, our digital signal would be stored as these numbers: 1, 10, 100, 111, 1000, 1001, 1000, 111, 100, 10, 1.

THE SCIENCE OF SOUND

This table shows how the numbers 1 to 8 are represented in binary form.

1	2	3	4	5	6	7	8
1	10	11	100	101	111	1000	1001

MODELING A MICROPHONE DIAPHRAGM

Try experimenting with this model of a microphone diaphragm.

You will need:
- **wax paper or strong tissue paper**
- **a can or large-mouthed jar**
- **a compass (optional)**
- **a rubber band**
- **poppy seeds, couscous, sesame seeds, or other small, light grains.**

Making it work

1 On your piece of wax paper or tissue paper, draw around the top of the can or jar.

2 If you have a compass, use it to draw a circle with a radius about 2 inches (5 centimeters) larger than the top of the can or jar. Otherwise, draw a rough circle with a radius about 2 inches (5 centimeters) larger than your can or jar.

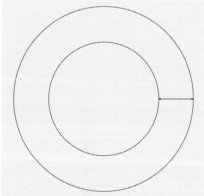

3 Cut out the larger circle.

4 Fit the wax paper circle over the top of the can or jar. Try to get the top as smooth and tight as possible. Use the rubber band to fasten it on. This is your microphone diaphragm.

5 Put a pinch or two of your seeds or grains on top of the diaphragm. Make sure they are spread out on the surface.

6 Now get close to the can or jar and sing a long note. Try not to blow on the surface as you sing. You should see the seeds or grains dance around on the surface.

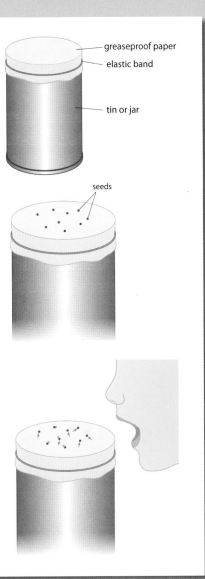

greaseproof paper

elastic band

tin or jar

seeds

Try some experiments

- Experiment with singing different notes. You could also try playing an instrument or your music system close to your can or jar. You will probably find that some notes work better than others. They make the wax paper vibrate more.
- If you can hold a long note, you may find that the seeds or grains move on the paper. Do you notice any patterns in how they move, or is it just random movement?

Storing the sound

A digital signal is a series of electrical 0s and 1s. This kind of signal can be stored on a computer hard drive, a CD, or a DVD.

Magnetic numbers

On a computer, the signal is stored on a magnetic hard drive. This is one or more magnetic disks that can spin very quickly. Each disk in a hard drive has one or more **read/write heads**. These are devices that can change the magnetism of a tiny part of the disk.

The digital sound signal is stored on the hard drive as a string of magnetic 0s and 1s. The 0 is no magnetic charge, and the 1 is a magnetic charge.

▲ This computer hard drive has a stack of six magnetic disks. The triangular device above the top disk is a read/write head.

Pits and bumps

On a CD or DVD, the 0s and 1s are stored in a slightly different way. On a CD, the 0s and 1s are stored as either flat areas or bumps on the CD surface. The bumps are incredibly tiny. They are created by a laser beam. The information on the CD is held in one long spiral track that runs from the outside of the CD, almost to the center. The whole track is almost 3 miles (5 kilometers) long!

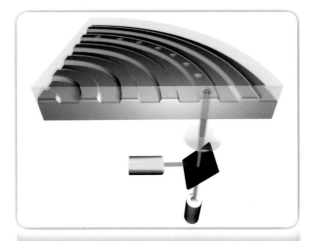

▲ To reveal the information on a CD or DVD, a laser shines a thin beam onto the surface's bumps and flat parts. The beam is reflected back from a flat part, but not from a bump.

SOUND FIRSTS

The earliest sound-recording device was called a phonograph. It was invented in 1877 by American inventor Thomas Edison. His recordings were made using a stylus (a kind of needle) to create a groove in a sheet of tinfoil. To play it back, the sheet of foil was wrapped around a cylinder. Another needle played the sounds back as the cylinder rotated.

▲ The first recording was of Edison saying the nursery rhyme "Mary Had a Little Lamb."

Alternative journeys

When the musicians record the sound of the wind and the thunder, they only capture a small part of the sound energy. What happens to the rest of it?

Spreading out

The noise of a thunderstorm can be heard several miles away. The sound waves spread out from the source of the sound like ripples in a pool. As the sound waves spread out, they become gradually weaker. This is because the same amount of energy is spread over a wider and wider area. Some of the sound energy also becomes heat, because the sound vibrations heat up the surrounding air slightly.

Did You Know?

It is not only thunderstorms that can break glass. In 2005, on a TV show called *Mythbusters*, rock singer Jaime Vendera broke a crystal glass with his voice by singing a high note.

▲ Rock singer Jaime Vendera breaks a glass using only his voice.

Eventually, the sound energy becomes so spread out that it becomes part of the general energy in the air. The energy is still there, but it is not very useful.

Shaking the walls

Usually, we don't think of sounds as actually doing anything. But really loud sounds can make things happen. When a storm is overhead, a clap of thunder can be 120 dB or more. This is close to the threshold (point) of pain. Sounds that are this loud have a lot of energy. The vibrations can be **transferred** to the walls and windows of nearby buildings, causing windows to break and walls to shake. The vibrations of the materials of the building also cause them to heat up.

▲ This high-speed photo shows a glass being shattered by sound from a loudspeaker.

What Happens in a Recording Studio?

The musicians have recorded the sounds of the storm. Now they go back to the recording studio to record the new song.

The different instruments are recorded as separate sound tracks. The singer adds the vocal track, then the sound engineer gets to work. She mixes together the different parts of the music and sections of the storm recording. She fades different tracks in and out at the right times. Finally, she gets the song sounding the way she wants.

➤ A guitarist and a singer record their tracks in a modern recording studio. The engineers monitor the sound on the computer screens.

Changing digital signals back to sounds

The sound engineer has stored the storm sounds on the hard drive of her computer. When she calls up the storm recording from the hard drive, the "read" head of the disk drive changes the magnetic patterns on the hard drive back into electrical signals. These travel through wires to the sound engineer's headphones.

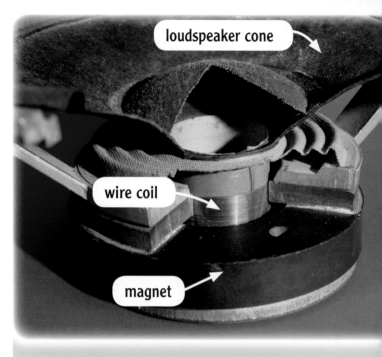

loudspeaker cone

wire coil

magnet

▲ This image shows the main parts of a loudspeaker.

Each ear of the headphones is a small loudspeaker. A loudspeaker is quite similar in design to a microphone. It has a magnet with an electric coil around it. The coil is attached to the cone of the loudspeaker.

Loudspeakers work in the opposite way from a microphone. When the electrical signal from the computer flows through the coil, it makes the coil move. The movement of the coil makes the loudspeaker cone vibrate, and this produces sounds.

DID YOU KNOW? In 2010, composer Eric Whitacre created his first "Virtual Choir" video on YouTube. He mixed together videos from 185 singers to make a single piece of choral music. The fourth "Virtual Choir" video, in 2014, involved mixing together the voices of nearly 6,000 people from around the world.

Boosting the signals

The recording of the song with the storm sounds on it has been released as part of an album. You buy a copy and download it. The music track that you download has none of the energy of the original thunderstorm. To listen to the sounds, you have to add energy to drive your sound system. This energy comes from an **amplifier**.

Increasing the sound

An amplifier boosts the power of an electrical signal. It relies on electronic devices called **transistors** that are part of the amplifier's microchip.

▲ Outdoor rock concerts need powerful amplifiers to make the sound loud enough for the whole audience to hear clearly.

The amplifier has two circuits. One has a very weak current that carries the electrical signal, and the other has a much larger current. The weak circuit controls the electricity flowing through the strong circuit, so that the electricity flow in the strong circuit mimics the signal in the weak circuit. This is like using a faucet to control the water flowing through a powerful hose. Turning the faucet doesn't take much energy, but it controls the flow of a large amount of water.

Space researchers use super-loud sound systems that are powerful enough to injure or even kill a person. The Large European Acoustic Facility has four sound horns that together can produce a sound level of 154 dB. It is used in testing satellites to make sure that they can withstand the sound levels in a rocket as it takes off. Another sound system in the United States—the WAS 3000—is very powerful. It can produce 165 dB of sound.

▲ A scientist sets up a test in the Large European Acoustic Facility. Behind him is one of the four large sound horns.

The final step: Into your ears

The recording of the thunderstorm that was made several weeks before is now part of a song that has spread around the world. You click on the track and the sound begins to play through the loudspeakers. In this final step of the energy journey, the sound of the storm travels from the loudspeakers to your ears.

How do our ears hear sound?

Before you can hear the sound of the storm, it has to get to your brain. Your ears are the sense organs that pick up the sound for your brain. The outside parts of your ears help to collect the sound and channel it into your **ear canals**. These are the small holes on the sides of your head. At the end of the ear canal is your **eardrum**. This is a thin membrane, similar to the diaphragm in a microphone. Sound waves traveling down the ear canal make the eardrum vibrate.

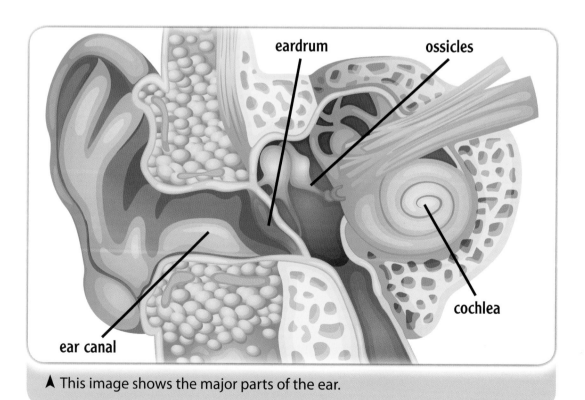

▲ This image shows the major parts of the ear.

▲ The fennec fox hunts at night. It relies on its sensitive hearing to help it find prey. The large external ears help by collecting more sound.

Behind the eardrum there are three tiny bones called the **ossicles**. These three bones focus the vibrations of the eardrum into a smaller area and make them more forceful.

The vibrations in the ossicles are passed on to another membrane. Behind this is a long, spiral tube, filled with fluid, called the **cochlea**. This is the part of the ear that detects the sounds.

In the cochlea, the sound vibrations cause movements in thousands of small hairs. These hairs are all connected to a nerve called the **auditory nerve**. The movements of the hairs send electrical signals along the auditory nerve to the brain. When the signals reach your brain, you hear the sounds in your head.

Alternative journeys

Your computer uses electrical energy to produce electrical signals. In your loudspeakers, these signals are turned into sound. However, a large amount of the electricity used in your computer does not become sound signals— it is wasted as heat.

Heating in circuits

In any electrical circuit, when electricity flows there is some **resistance** to the flow. Electrical resistance is like friction within the circuit, and like friction it produces heat. The large processor microchips in your computer produce quite a lot of resistance, and so they get hot. If the microchips in the computer get too hot, they do not work correctly. So, the extra heat has to be carried away.

▲ This combination of a fan and several heat sinks is used to cool a computer graphics processor.

▲ Powerful computer systems like this one produce too much heat to be cooled with fans. They use a liquid cooling system instead.

Most computers are cooled using **heat sinks** and fans. A heat sink is a block of metal split into many thin cooling fins. Metal is a good conductor of heat, and it carries heat away from the microchips. The computer's fan then blows the warm air from the heat sink out of the computer. Most computers have several large microchips, so they have several cooling fans.

THE SCIENCE OF SOUND

The central processing units (CPUs) of computers carry out millions of **operations** every second. Because of the way these operations are carried out, many involve "throwing away" electricity, and this electricity becomes heat. Researchers at the Massachusetts Institute of Technology (MIT), in Cambridge, Massachusetts, have found a new way to do the operations in a CPU that avoids producing waste heat. This could make future computers much more efficient.

What Have We Learned About Sound?

In this energy journey, we have seen how kinetic energy, chemical energy, potential energy, and electrical energy can be transformed into sound energy, and how sound travels as waves. We have also followed sounds as they are transformed into kinetic energy, electrical energy, patterns of magnetism, and heat energy.

In this journey, there were many energy transformations, when the energy changed from one form into another. An example is when the kinetic energy of wind is transformed into sound energy when it causes a taut rope or wire to vibrate.

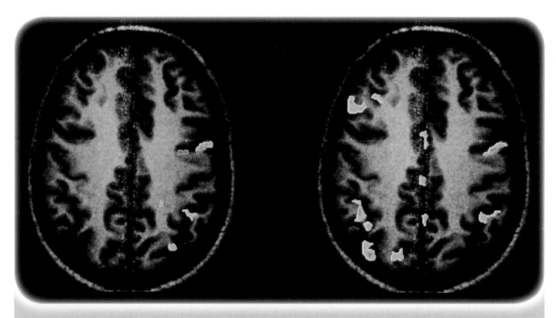

▲ The real end of our energy journey is in your brain, where the sounds that you hear are processed. The yellow/orange patches on this EEG scan are areas of electrical activity in a human brain.

In experiments in 2012, scientists found that combining electrical brainwaves with measurements of blood flow through the brain produced pleasant "brain music." In 2014, the New York artist Lisa Park created a performance in which the music was created directly from her brainwaves. In the performance, she also uses trays of water placed over loudspeakers. The water leaps and sprays in response to the sound.

▲ New York artist Lisa Park performs her "brainwaves" piece, *Eunoia*.

There were also some energy transfers, when the energy stays in the same form but is transferred from one place to another. An example of this is when the vibrations of the eardrum are transferred to the tiny bones inside the ear.

Finally, we have seen how some kinds of energy are more useful than others. When heat, vibration, or other energy becomes very spread out, we cannot use it to do things or make things happen.

Indestructible energy

Across the whole energy journey, we have found that energy is never lost or destroyed. It sometimes seems that way, but if you investigate, you find that the energy has simply changed to another form. Energy really is indestructible!

Glossary

amplifier electronic device that makes a sound signal louder

amplitude height of a wave

analog sound or other electrical signal that varies continuously, rather than in steps like a digital signal

auditory nerve nerve that carries sound signals from the ear to the brain

binary number system that uses only zeroes and ones

charge (electrical) excess of positively charged or negatively charged particles

chemical potential energy energy stored in the chemical bonds that hold the atoms of a substance together

cochlea (inner ear) part of the ear that turns sound vibrations into nerve signals

conductor material that allows heat or electricity to pass through it easily

conservation of energy scientific law saying that energy cannot be created or destroyed

decibel unit for measuring the loudness of sound

diaphragm (microphone) thin membrane found in a microphone that vibrates in response to sound

digital information information stored in the form of numbers, usually binary numbers

digital signal sound or other electrical signal made up of digital information

ear canal passage that leads from the outer ear opening to the eardrum

eardrum part of the ear that vibrates in response to sound

elastic potential energy energy stored by either stretching or compressing an elastic material (a material that bounces back after it has been stretched or squeezed)

electrical signal variations in the current or voltage of a flow of electricity that carry information

electricity type of energy produced by charged particles traveling along a wire

frequency the frequency of a wave is the number of wave peaks or troughs that pass a stationary point in one second

fulgurite tube-like or root-like formation in sand or rock, caused by lightning

gravitational potential energy energy stored in an object that is raised above Earth's surface

harmonics musical notes that are higher or lower than the main note (the one you hear), which give a sound its particular quality

heat sink device designed to cool electronic circuits by carrying away heat

hertz unit for measuring frequency (1 Hz = 1 wave per second)

insulator material that does not allow heat or electricity to pass easily through it

kinetic energy movement energy

operation (computer) calculation done by the central processing unit (CPU) of a computer

oscilloscope instrument that can show sounds or electrical signals as traces on a screen

ossicle one of three tiny bones in the ear that transfer vibrations from the eardrum to the cochlea

pitch how high or low a musical note (or a sound) is

potential energy energy that is stored in some way

read/write head small device that moves across the face of a computer hard disk, reading the patterns of magnetism on the disk and turning them to electrical signals, or turning electrical signals into magnetic patterns on the disk

resistance (electrical) kind of "frictional force" in an electric circuit that resists the flow of electricity

sample measure an analog signal many times per second in order to create a digital signal

shock wave sharp change of pressure traveling through the air, caused by an explosion or by something moving faster than the speed of sound

sonic boom loud sound produced when an aircraft or other vehicle travels faster than the speed of sound

supersonic faster than the speed of sound

transfer (energy) when energy stays in the same form (for example, kinetic energy), but is passed from one substance to another

transform (energy) when energy changes from one form to another— for example, from light into chemical energy

transistor electronic component in an amplifier that actually amplifies the electric signal

ultrasound sound waves with frequencies above the highest-pitched sounds that humans can hear

vibration rapid back and forth movement

volt unit of electrical force

wave kind of energy or motion produced by back and forth movement

wavelength distance between the top of one wave and the top of the next one

Find Out More

Books

Carlson Berne, Emma. *Loud! Sound Energy* (Energy Everywhere). New York: PowerKids, 2013.

Challoner, Jack. *Sound and Light* (Hands-On Science). New York: Kingfisher, 2013.

Claybourne, Anna. *Ear-Splitting Sounds and Other Vile Noises* (Disgusting and Dreadful Science). New York: Crabtree, 2013.

Hartman, Eve, and Wendy Meshbesher. *Light and Sound* (Sci-Hi). Chicago: Raintree, 2010.

Hewitt, Sally. *Amazing Sound* (Amazing Science). New York: Crabtree, 2008.

Web sites

www.landspeedrecord.org/thrust-ssc-andy-green/

Here you can read facts about the record-breaking car, and about the record-breaking flight that happened 50 years earlier.

www.nationalgeographic.com/features/96/lightning/

You can learn more about lightning and read stories about lightning strikes on this web site.

www.pbs.org/benfranklin/shocking/

This web site has an animation that takes you through Benjamin Franklin's discoveries about lightning.

www.ted.com/talks/eric_whitacre_a_virtual_choir_2_000_voices_strong.html

This is the story of how musician Eric Whitacre created a choir on YouTube.

www.youtube.com/watch?v=qNf9nzvnd1k

The clip on this web site has a soundtrack that goes through the whole range of human hearing, from 20 Hz to 20,000 Hz.

Place to visit

The Exploratorium

Pier 15, San Francisco, California 94111

The Exploratorium is a great place to visit to find out about any science or technology topic, including sound, and to have fun with hands-on exhibits. Look on the web site for details about upcoming special events, shows, and exhibitions.

www.exploratorium.edu

Further research

There is a lot more to learn about sound. Here are some ideas for topics to research.

- "Everyone hears things differently." Is this true? Design an experiment to test it out. You could use the human audio spectrum on the YouTube web site listed on page 46.
- What is a Rubens tube? Do some research to find out about this amazing piece of physics equipment. Do a "show-and-tell" for your friends.
- Acoustic levitation: Is it real? Look up acoustic levitation on the Internet. Is it real or a trick? What could it be used for?
- Making musical instruments: Find out more about cigar box guitars.
- Who is Felix Baumgartner? What was his amazing record-breaking feat?

Index